Vid's Viddles

Daily Vitamins for the Soul

Vid Lamonte' Buggs Jr.

4-U-Nique Publishing
A Series of VLB/VBJ Enterprises, LLC

4-U-Nique Publishing books may be purchased for educational,
business, or sales promotional use. For information, please email:
info@4-U-Nique Publishing.com

First Edition

Cover Design By: 4-U-Nique Publishing

Cover Art By: Dollar Photo Club

Library of Congress Cataloging-in-Publication Data

ISBN-13: 978-0692826270

ISBN-10: 0692826270

This Book is dedicated to my family:

Andrea, my son, Dominique Mikail, and my daughter, Sofia Lyn.

To the reader, this book is for you. Remember everything you need is already within you. **Shine Bright**!

Contents

FOREWORD
by Berton R. Newbill

When I first met Vid, it was at the South Tampa YMCA on the basketball court. That is where our friendship began, on a small enclosed, rectangle of about 80-90 square feet bounded by black tape and two-story walls, full of redirected dreams and long-lasting memories. It is from within the confines of this structure that our friendship expanded well beyond the bourne of those court markings and the gym walls. Vid is a deep thinker, a reader, and a life-long learner. His writings reflect this and a lot more. I thought he was a pretty good baller who was obviously playing "down" to the level of competition on the court at 5:30 a.m. on Mondays, Wednesdays, and Fridays. (Yes, we play at 5:30 a.m., three times a week…regularly.) When I walked into the gym and saw him stretching, I knew that I had to up my game in order to stay on the court whether I played with him or against him. He inspired me to play better, to reach a level that I did not know I had in me. He elevated all of our games. This is what Vid's Viddles does. It makes you think, it makes you look, then re-look at things that you may have seen but didn't observe. It challenges you to look at yourself, to look at the world and your place in it, to see where we all fit in or maybe not. When I read this book, I felt like I was sitting on the bench after a few games and talking with Vid as we stretched and prepared for the rest of the day; it was thought-provoking and reflective, stimulating and inspirational, yet not intrusive. So I invite you to take a break and sit on the gym floor to stretch and rejuvenate your mind and spirit with a friend.

Introduction

What is the purpose for me writing a book about life and its fortunes? I am writing this book because I see people not understanding what life is about or the reasons for their struggles. Also, I want to show people that no matter what culture, race, or where they are from, we as humans all have problems. I want to expose those problems to every kind of person.

I came to the conclusion to write a book, because people of all colors, sex, and creeds have asked me for advice. People are intrigued by my philosophy, my psychology, my sayings, and my analogies. They asked me to write a book to help others in the world.

I am no wiser than any person in the world. However, I do have understandings in life, actions, and struggles, even at my relative younger age. Why, the readers are asking? The reason is, I sit back, observe, and analyze things around me; every action, reaction, and the world itself. Keep in mind that I am an ordinary person, just one who has been through a lot and seen things from a lot of angles.

In this book I will discuss life, pain, struggle, success, relationships, death, race, the government, the world, and other things. One topic I will not discuss is religion. The reason is there are many religions and even if two people share the same religion they will have different ideas, thoughts, and beliefs about that religion. Plus, what I have to discuss will just get confused if religion is involved.

What I want from this book is for people to understand, think, observe, and analyze. These things are what I observe through my experiences, and everyone observes differently through their experiences. This is what life is about, learning and understanding from one's experiences.

Part One
Vitamin A: Important for Good Vision

Monday

It's Monday! Most of us complain about having to wake up to go to work. I say instead of complaining, be thankful that, *1. You are waking up, 2. You have a job, and 3. Although you may not realize it you are making a difference in the world.* Do not start your week off in the wrong direction with negative thoughts. Start it off with positive thoughts and the week will be positive. Each day greet at least 10 people with a smile and a hug (10 is easy). You should go up to at least 3 strangers in the day and give them a hug. Put your ego, fear and pride aside. If you can do this you can do anything you put your mind to. We often are held back from achieving things because of *Ego, Fear* and *Pride.*

Control

What is the meaning of *Life*, *Love*, *Passion* and *Art*? The meanings of these things are whatever you want them to be; it is your perception of your experiences which makes you and shapes your life. Stop for a few moments and take the time to see the beauty of this world; the smell of flowers, the singing of birds, the actual taste of an orange, the touch of a raindrop, and the feel of unconditional love. Sit back and realize your perception is yours; it is not the perception of the world.

On my travel to and from Cincinnati, I started to really appreciate the airplane; the great minds behind it and the gift that spawned the idea (the birds of the sky). We rarely stop to think in our busy lives, how wonderful life is. Here I am thousands of feet in the air, traveling hundreds of miles per hour, over clouds, houses, and earth. I am breathing in recycled air and there are at least 100 individuals sharing the experience with me. We are one group. Some are scared; some are fearless like myself and others are tired. Some engage in conversation while others listen to music, read a book, and/or work on their laptops.

The most amazing part was we were all in harmony. There were no worries of race, religion, or political ideas. You can say we let our own perceptions, just for a few hours play second fiddle. Once the plane landed, we all thanked the pilot, the crew and said our best wishes to one another. We stepped off the plane back to our individual worlds of worry and hurry.

Why do we worry and hurry? You can only control what is in your hands, and if it is in your hands, do the best you can with what you have. Once it's out of your hands it's gone. The hurrying will cause you to miss life's treasures: the essence of a conversation, the sound of a song.

Search

It is better to search for the truth instead of depending on and believing others' words as the truth. When you always depend on the words of others, you will be deceived time and time again. Successful people are not lazy. They search for the answers to the questions that intrigue them instead of going by what people tell them. Searching for the truth will always make you free, but depending on others' words as truth will make you a slave forever.

Focus

Do not focus on the person I/you were, focus on the person that I am/you are. Learn from yesterday, enjoy today and plan for the future. Each day we must face change and change is great - *After Night, Day comes, the Rain falls and the Sun shines making a Rainbow; Seasons bring growth.* - Don't be scared of the change that is in you because change is always happening around you.

Don't Look Back

Keep your eyes on the prize and never look back. When you look back you lose focus on where you are going and may get discouraged by the lengths you have traveled. Keep focusing and don't look back.

Future/Present

Your future is determined by what you are doing now, in the present.

View of the World

Your view of the truth or the world does not make your view or truth *Universal*. Your view may be tainted, like looking at the world through a dirty or tinted window. When you go outside or open the window the view is always clearer.

Blessings

Stop looking for that one major sign or blessing. We need to realize that signs or blessings do not come in the shape or form we always want them. We also have to realize there are blessings and signs all around us, every moment. The signs in the *Great Books* and in *History* should be all one needs to know that they will be blessed. The story of Egypt and Israel serves as a guide for knowing your prayers will be answered.

Reap What You Sow

Reap What You Sow

Positivity cannot come forth if a positive seed is not planted.

Love cannot be received if love isn't given.

Answers will not come if questions aren't asked.

The Search for Happiness

The search for happiness starts within you. You cannot expect material possessions or another being to make you happy. Happiness is so simple to find; yet, for some of us, it's hard to achieve. I hear people say all the time, "If I had a million dollars, I'd be set". My question is, what if you never get a million dollars? Will you live life unhappy? The keys and answers to all things lie within you. *The Secret is – there really is no Secret.* You don't need any books to discover this.

Signs

People look for signs and get frustrated and lose faith when they do not see the signs that they are looking for. One can only blame himself or herself for not seeing the signs. Most of us are conditioned to only look for signs in the way we want them to come to us. However, when you do that you miss out on the *True Signs*.

Perception

Your perception is not the world's perception. The world has been here long before you and will be here long after you are gone. How you see things does not mean others have to see things your way or feel the way you do. For example, when people see things not going exactly in my favor, they will end up saying, "Well, that sucks". When I reply, "Not really", they say, "Well, I know you are frustrated because I would be". Truth of the matter is I don't really get frustrated about anything. There is reasoning in all things and everything that *God* has created is for good. Even if it hurts a little, it's the true meaning of *Tough Love*.

Part Two
Vitamin B Complex: Important for the Body's Energy and Brain Function

Take Action

Everyone has problems, but those who complain are not changing anything. Instead of complaining about your issues, you should take that energy and fix the issues at hand. What are you going to do? Take action and be proactive or be like most of the world and wait to react and be reactive?

Do As You Feel

I find that most people say they don't know what they want to do with their life. However, in most cases they really do realize what they want to do in life. They just do not understand how to achieve all the goals they want to accomplish and do not know which direction to go. My advice is to make a sound plan; balance your time wisely and do everything that you wish to do in your life.

Focused

Don't focus on winning; focus on not losing. Most think the two are the same, but they aren't the same at all. When focusing on winning one may take for granted or overlook the little important facts, details, things, etc. However, when focusing on not losing, one focuses on every detail.

Remember to give back and do some charity work. You will feel better and make the world a better place. Remember, no matter how low you are, there are people who are lower or have it worse. You cannot receive anything with a closed hand but an open hand receives many things.

Open Your Mind

Take the negative and turn it into a positive.
Everything that happens is a learning experience.
Negative experiences help you become wiser and
stronger. As people, we have to battle the ups and
downs of life in order to grow and become a person of
higher form. Don't focus on the negative side of a
situation, focus on the positive side. Learning and
growing is always positive.

Many of us limit ourselves because we do not open up
our minds. I was talking to someone, and they kept
telling me every *excuse* for why they can't do
something. After rebutting, she finally admitted that
she hadn't done things because she is scared. You
know the World is not as big as people make it. If you
use your mind, you can become global with whatever
you do. Ever wonder why people say, "It's a Small

World"? It is because everyone knows the same people; six degrees of separation. The key is finding those five degrees that separate you. It may seem that I'm going off subject but if you really think about it, I'm not. The point is simple, use your mind, be open and you can do anything. People seem to not be the best at what they do or live up to their potential because they are scared of *Change*, *Challenges* and/or *Doing Their Best*. Just know with an open mind you will be able to conquer the *World*.

Positive Thinking

When you wake up in the morning, your first thought should be one of thankfulness because you get to see another day. Next you should have positive thoughts about the day. Positive thinking brings positive situations. Negativity is a magnet that attracts negative from all areas. You will start to get the problems of others laid upon you. Take the *you* or *I* out of the world because the world is bigger than just you and I. When we take out the *you* or *I*, we are able to accomplish more. God has made the world just the way it is supposed to be. It's up to each one of us to make the world a better place. Start with yourself and help others. If you do not truly love yourself, you cannot love your neighbor and change will not come.

Reflection and Relaxation

We tend to overwork ourselves; we do not give the body, mind, soul, and spirit time to relax and reflect. This causes one to wear down, stress, and carry on negative energy. God did not intend for us to work and stress our life away. My challenge to you all is for an hour a day, relax and reflect. Relaxation does not mean going to sleep or looking at TV. It means to sit down in quiet time, by a pool, beach, in the woods, park or at home, just you and the four walls with no worries on your mind.

Taking a Break

Most of us never take a break to settle our thoughts, relax and reflect. We are so busy with the demands of the world; we put doing things for others in front of taking a break for ourselves. If you continue to do so, you will not have the life and the happiness that you want. Take a break from everything for as little as an hour, it helps you reflect and be at peace. I do not mean taking a break by cleaning the house and listening to music. I mean take a break with no noise, just you and silence. This is when you truly get to know yourself. At least once a week for an hour we should take a break from it all.

Part Three

Vitamin C: Important for the Body's Healing and Absorption

Chinks in the Armor

Chinks in the Armor!!! More often than not when the Devil cannot get to you, he will try to work through people who are around you. This can work in many ways, however, the one I want to focus on is when people do not believe in you and try to hold you down. Most do so due to jealousy or fear, although, most of the time they do not know what they are doing. Some people do not want you to grow because they are scared that you will leave them behind. Others may not want you to grow because you are reaching new levels and it shows them it is possible for them to also reach higher levels. They are content in not going hard; it's not that they cannot reach higher levels, it's that they don't want to. Avoid these people when they are spewing negativity around you. Keep your focus, go your way and keep reaching for higher levels.

Ending the Cycle

If you are continually going through a cycle and cannot find out how to end it, look no further than yourself. You are going through a continuous situation because you are failing to learn the lessons that are needed to get out of the cycle. Stop looking and placing blame on others and take responsibility first.

Letting Go

Letting go of dead weight. If you are being drained by the actions of others who are around you, it's time to let them go and do your own thing. Surround yourself with people who will uplift you.

Don't Let Your Problems Keep You Down

We all have problems. Don't let your problems, issues and circumstances stop you from doing what you want and are meant to do. There are reasons and consequences for everything. Learn from your experiences and move on. Don't let anything hold you back or down from being happy and your true destiny.

Problems and Issues

The problems and issues that we all go through are not just for our benefit, but also the benefit of others. No one's issues are unique. Dealing with your issues helps you grow and helps others who are going or will go through the same issues you are going through. Your situations and how you deal with them can be someone else's foresight before their hindsight.

Regrets

One should not have any regrets. Many of us look back on the choices or mistakes we made in our lives. Upon looking back we feel sorry for making past choices and we wish we could change the outcome. However, we should not do this because in doing so one would change the person who they have become. Our choices and mistakes help mold us into who we are. No matter what, there is something that we can learn from every choice and mistake that we have made. A bad choice or mistake is like getting off the wrong exit on the interstate of life. You may get off on the wrong exit but that particular exit holds another experience in life, from which you can learn and appreciate. Live, and learn without having regrets.

Share

What is the purpose in having love, wisdom, happiness and knowledge if one does not share them with the world? Love, wisdom, happiness and knowledge are meant to be shared with others. In keeping these things within, one is keeping the manifestation of peace and love from others.

The Power of Forgiveness.

A strong person is not measured by their physical strength. They are measured by their faith, patience, perseverance, and forgiveness of others. Forgiveness is key; how can one expect to be forgiven for their mistakes if one is not able to forgive another for theirs? We must learn to love others and ourselves the same. You will see that a person's past does not define the person in the present. Yes, the past helped shape the person of today but are you the same person now that you were last month? Indeed you are not because you have gone through many experiences good and bad. All for the better. A person who holds grudges has a weak heart, weak mind, and weak spirit. When one holds grudges one is harboring negative energy, which leads to stress. More importantly, harboring negative energy many times leads to evil. Being forgiving is like a breath of fresh air.

Truth

The truth comes in many forms. The truth is often there even though we cannot see nor understand it. Next time you dispute the truth because it's outside of your understanding or is improbable, take a step back and analyze the truth.

The Great men, women, and Prophets were punished and killed for the truths they told because no one believed them. Many years later, mankind marvels at their words and wisdom, often saying they were great people who lived way before their time.

Part Four
Vitamin D: Important for the Body's Growth and Strengthening

Breaking Out of Your Comfort Zone.

Do things you wouldn't normally do or something you never have done in your life. You will learn more about yourself and others. Walk up and converse with a stranger. By doing this you will break stereotypes because you will see how similar we all are and learn from each other's differences.

Don't Follow the Trend

Do not follow the trend of others, be your own person. People may not believe what you are for or the things you are attempting to accomplish are good moves or *cool*. However, most of the people are just waiting for a special person to come along, a person who is genuinely "*them*" no matter what others think; a person who rages against the machine (government, trends, majority, etc.). Be that special person. Remember what history has taught us; the views and moves that are not popular now, seem to be the right moves/views later and become popular over time.

Faith/Positive

Be faithful and remain positive. No matter what happens, everything will work itself out. Sometimes it just takes time for what you want and need to prosper. Keeping faith and remaining positive will make whatever you desire (as long as it is of good nature) attainable.

Leader/Servant

A leader is a servant of the people, a leader acknowledges when they are wrong and they are humble when they are right. A leader learns from his/her defeats, but wins are never good enough for a leader. Leader or follower, which one are you?

Redefinition of Me

There comes a time in everyone's life when they must wake up and change the person they are to the person they want to become. This may include exploring new horizons, becoming more open-minded, facing fears instead of running from them, and becoming more serious about life instead of partying it away. We may also leave people behind to make ourselves better (redefine). You are what you think you are, and you are what you do; so if you hang around negative people you yourself are a negative person. "Birds of a Feather flock together", so if you are trying to become the person you want to be in the future, you have to redefine who you are now.

Self-Realization

Anything is possible if you look deep down inside
yourself to find the answers. Struggle comes to make you
stronger. Every obstacle brings character and strength.
Do not let your emotions define your character unless
your emotions and character are of positivity.

The Limit

The sky isn't the limit; the limit is as limitless as the sky. In fact, the limit is in your mind. Appreciate all that you have but reach for more. Never get discouraged by the negative results of your progress (ex. rejection) but use it to fuel you towards achieving your goals. Remember one positive can outshine and overcome many negatives.

Timing

Timing is everything; we've heard this time and time again. However, most people really do not understand what it means nor do they apply it to their lives. People want things when they want them. Timing is the key because if we get things too soon we may not cherish them. If we get them too late we may not need them anymore. The next time you are cursing out a slow driver in front of you, Stop. Thank God and the driver because that person may have held you up a split second to avoid something that could've been tragic to you.

Part Five
Vitamin E: Important for the Body's Integrity

Be Yourself

Many of us are not being our true selves. We are busy trying to be who others want us to be. Continuously, we complain because we aren't happy with life. It is your choice to do, be and act how you want. People are scared to be themselves because they do not want to face criticism. I've been weird throughout my life. People criticized me for dating outside my race; the kinds of music I enjoy; the different ways I dress; going places that others felt was weird and doing things that others were afraid to try. Those who laughed at me then admire me now for standing out from the crowd.

Who wants to do the same thing over and over again, or the same as everyone else? Truth be told, no one does but most of us are scared to be different. Live outside the box and enjoy life. You are the master of your personal universe, so live life how you want it to be; you have to write your own chapters in life. If you don't love the job you are at, work somewhere else. Do not let your life be consumed by meditating on how much you hate your job and not looking forward to going back to work. Be yourself; take care of yourself first and stop being what everyone else wants you to be. Remember, people who live outside the box are more intriguing.

Be Happy

Be happy and content with what you have. Do not be greedy and spiteful. If you do you may end up losing that which you already have.

Pay It Forward

Pay it forward; every good deed given is a good deed received.

The Cause

Many times we follow people and are inspired by people because of the *Cause* they are fighting for or leading. However, we are quick to stop following that person and stop believing in the *Cause* because the person who is leading it has messed up in his/her life along the way. We forget that no one is perfect. More importantly, if a person's fall from glory finds you not fighting for the *Cause* anymore, then you really didn't believe in the *Cause* nor were you fighting for it at all. If Dr. Martin Luther King Jr. had fallen as a man and the people who followed him stopped fighting for equality because of their leader's fall, where would we be today? Which is greater, the person leading the Cause or the Cause itself?

Wait for No One and Never Settle for Less.

If you wait for people to help you get to where you want to go in life, time may pass you by and you may never achieve the goals you set for yourself. We all need help from time to time but you should never depend on others to help you solve your problems. You should always have back up plans. The fact of the matter is, other people have issues and other goals that are more important than helping you with yours.

Never settle for less. When you settle for less you will never be truly satisfied or happy. You will continuously wonder what if and may have regrets. Strive for the best and nothing more because when you believe, you will achieve. It takes time but it's worth it.

War/Peace

War doesn't bring *Peace* and hate doesn't bring *Love*. Two wrongs do not make a right or bring justice. Be the person that you want the world to be. Stay focused and positive and great things will come. Great things take time, but what is time in the infinite spiritual world? Separate the mental from the body and you will achieve your goals.

Whatever You Want to Be

Whatever you want to be in life, ride the wave to become that person. Do not let anyone take your goals and dreams away from you. What may seem impossible and improbable to others is possible and probable to you as long as you are headstrong and focused.

What's Fun?

People have a misunderstanding of what is fun. I guess it's the forces of negativity that trick people into this way of thinking. Many people think they need some kind of substance to make their days or nights fun. Which isn't true. The substances are giving you a false sense of fun. Many times after a night of drinking you hear people say, "I shouldn't have done that".

More importantly, you can be about God and have fun. People have the notion that because you are living life right you are not having fun. If you want to have fun in life, you must try new things. Many people complain there is nothing fun to do and they are tired of doing the same things over and over again, yet, they will not try anything new. What it all comes down to is you have to make your own fun.

97

Part Six
Vitamin K: Important for Clotting Blood and Protecting the Heart

Inside You

Focus on the invisible person who is inside your body because that is the true you. Focus less on the physical being, the jewelry, clothes, shoes, etc. The physical does not define who you are; it is simply the cover to the book when what's inside is what truly matters.

Love and Respect

I used to ask myself; why do people treat others so badly when you are supposed to love your neighbor as you do yourself and treat others as you want to be treated? Now I realize the love I imagined people had for themselves does not exist. They cannot love their neighbors because they don't even know how to love themselves. If you don't respect yourself, how are you going to respect others?

It is said that the believers will endure long-suffering. I once looked at this saying one-sidedly. I looked at it simply as, we (believers) would be persecuted, accused, hated, be in constant war between *Spirit* and *Flesh*, good and evil, morals and materials. This is still true. However, I now see another side to the saying, that the believers will endure long-suffering because they realize the light is what makes them happy; however, they are sad because they see so many people living in the dark.

Love All

Love you all, this means the *World*. Because loving you means loving me and loving me means loving you. We can't truly love the divine *Spirit* (God) until we love all, forgive all, and have peace with all. We all are made in God's image, no matter our differences. No thought is original because it is which comes from *Him*. Even the tests, they are all meant to bring us closer to *Him*.

The Future

People complain about the younger generation; the troubles they are going through and the troubles that they are causing. My question is, what have you done to help the situation get better? I know what we have done to make the situation get worse. We have simply talked about the problems but ignored them at the same time.

Uncensored

Rain falls, the sun shines, and the flowers grow. Problems and issues arise, but it all makes us grow. When the sun shines back on you, the problems and issues of yesterday make your inner and outer self glow as bright as the sun. Why treat our problems of today as if it is the end of our lives? If that is true, then we each died a thousand deaths. In dying a thousand deaths, we lived a thousand and one times, each life better than the other.

Secondly, why do we continue to judge one another? To judge is to form opinions about others. We all must understand that opinions are not facts. Furthermore, we have all been judged by others, how did that make you feel? If someone doesn't like to be judged why would that someone go around and judge others? Some people judge others by what they eat, what they believe in and what they wear. One does not realize what a person has been through or is going through to act the way they act. I have many times been judged for the worse because of my skin, which I do not understand. How people of color (all color) continue to judge others, knowing the judgment of others led to their own discrimination.

Third, Love. What is this Love? Most people have no idea what love is. Most people love because of how that person/thing makes them feel or what they do for that person. This isn't love at all. This is having pleasure for a person/thing because it attends to their desires. Once that person or thing hurts them, they do not love them or it anymore. Love is not conditional, love is forgiving, and love makes a person put away their pride. Love is something one has for a person/thing, whether the object of that love knows, just because it's a creation of God or a brother/sister.

The light shines on you all, but some people are in the dark because they keep their eyes closed.

Part Seven

Essential Minerals: Important for the Body's Growth, Development, and Maintaining Normal Health

1. Faith, Patience and Perseverance will knock down walls and move mountains.

2. Strength is not in numbers. Strength is in Faith.

3. Isn't it great that when you are spiritually tuned in that everything in the universe is connected?

4. Most people need to see things in the physical to have faith. When in truth, we should have faith in things before we see them. Putting your trust in the unseen is what we call faith.

5. We plant seeds with faith that they will grow and bring forth fruits. We go to sleep with the faith of seeing another day. Yet tomorrow is not promised nor do we see tomorrow or the fruits of the seeds in the physical. Why do most people need to see things in the physical, in order to believe they will come true? If a person has the faith that they will get a raise, food, or whatever, it shall prosper. My friends have faith and see it prosper.

6. Each night before one goes to sleep, one should reflect on their day and what they learned during the day. If one hasn't learned anything new that day, the day has almost become a waste.

7. The worst pain is not the pain that is caused by another person. The worst pain is the pain caused by one's self. A person can deny the pain that is caused by another; but a person cannot avoid the pain of self-infliction.

8. What separates an idiot from a wise person are the things that a wise person has learned through their experiences and mistakes. A wise person uses what they learned to avoid making the same mistakes again, while an idiot does not care to use what is learned. Therefore, he will experience things over and over again only to make the same mistakes again and again.

9. Arrogance is having confidence without being humble. Confidence is assurance of one's self while being humble.

10. Struggles make a person stronger; struggles build character. They may seem impossible to get through when going through them, however, once a person gets through them it feels as if they are on top of the world.

11. A wise person educates but does not flaunt their wisdom. A fool flaunts their "wisdom" only to show they do not know anything at all.

12. A successful leader is one who followed before leading. Thus, learning from the mistakes and success of those who came before them.

13. A leader is a leader because they step up to take charge and fight for what they believe in. They accept the fact that they are wrong when they are wrong, but they are humble when they are right.

14. People who hate the positive, but love the negative only do so because they are not making a positive

difference. They are jealous of the people who are making a positive difference.

15. What separates a man and woman from a girl and boy is not the age but the person's maturity level.

16. There are two kinds of love. The first love is loving a person only if all circumstances are right. The second love is the love one has for a person no matter what the circumstances are.

17. The simplest things are the most complex because we question the simple things in search of the reason that makes it more difficult to understand. For example, questioning the meaning of life or questioning why a person loves/likes another person.

18. There is a difference between complex and hard or simple and easy. Things can be complex but easy, simple but hard, complex but hard or simple and easy.

19. Just because you do not see the truth does not mean the truth does not exist. For the truth will come out of the dark and hit you in the head when you least expect.

20. Always stay positive and treat people well because you never know what a smile can do for a person. Your smile could be the last thing a person sees before death. Your smile can save a life, change a stereotype, or an attitude. It is a warm and pleasant feeling to look back on life when it is winding down in the last seconds and your final vision is a warm smile.

21. At the end of a day, one should reflect on what they did that day. If one has not learned at least one thing they did not know before that day, then the day is a waste and nothing was accomplished. We learn from our day-to-day experiences and interactions with others.

22. There will come a time in a person's life when that person will have to compromise himself for something or someone they want or love. This compromise does not mean the person will change who they are. A mature person will know how to compromise without changing who or what they are.

23. One must understand that when one chooses between things, one will lose something, thus, making decisions or choices hard to make.

24. People tend to not try because they are scared to fail. However, when one does not try and gives up one has already failed.

25. Everyone wants to be successful. However, some people tend not to try to succeed because they do not know what to do after they become successful, how to stay successful, or if their successes bring happiness.

26. Success is not determined by how much money a person has; it is determined by the goals one has met and the happiness in that person's life.

27. To have wisdom, knowledge, and love is pointless if one does not share them with others.

28. One can try to educate a person who has a closed mind and heart, but that person will never be educated until they open their mind and heart.

29. We all are looking for freedom. Freedom comes only when one frees his mind, body and soul.

30. We all search to make history; however, we end up making "his" story. Find yourself and make your story and your own glory.

31. Do your best not to stress over things. Whatever happens will happen. Things are put into our hands to control. We control those things the best we can. The things that are not in our hands, we should not stress over because we have no control over them. That is putting faith in God, but also having faith in yourself.

32. In life a person is always a student. It doesn't matter how long they've lived or how long they've done something.

33. Rule the world! Do not let the world rule you.

34. People can be interested in and/or in love with someone but not even know who they are. This is hard to believe but simple to understand. This is so because all your life you have had this format of what you want/look for in a person, then you meet that person and you fall in love instantly. Why? It is because you found the person who is everything you envisioned and more.

35. *Being a Soldier of God* on a surface level sucks. You see people who live life wrong; getting all life's rewards while on earth. *Being a Soldier of God* one cannot live life wrong even when one tries. Even though the *Soldier of God* is not getting the rewards of this world, the *Soldier* gets rewarded in the afterlife. This makes being a *Soldier of God* the greatest thing in the world. Those who are not are the ones who are suffering because they are blinded by the devil's work and rewards.

36. One should never become comfortable with what one has accomplished. One should keep trying harder and try to improve each day.

37. A person should look back each day and see how they improved and became a better person from the previous day.

38. Flirting with temptation is like walking into a lion's den and not expecting to get bit.

39. Fighting wars does not and will not ever create peace. Peace comes from love and understanding.

40. Your kind giving will never be forgotten. It is said, "A closed hand does not receive, but an open giving hand will receive continually". Give with gratitude for you may not know who is among you. Receive with a kind heart for every gift is a blessing.

41. You cannot love or make anyone else happy and they cannot make you happy until you love yourself and are happy with yourself.

42. There are many paths to take in this journey we call life; some are easier, some are harder; some are longer and some are shorter. Each has different views and scenery. However, we all end up at the same place no matter which path we take in finding our way back home.

43. We all must face our fears in order to realize there was nothing to fear in the first place, allowing us to get on with our lives and live our lives to the fullest. It is like falling to the bottom and realizing the fall wasn't that bad. How can one climb to the top of the mountain with the fear of falling?

44. The start of making the world a better place is to better yourself and lend a helping hand each day.

45. Change is not bad. It is compromising the person you are that is bad. If one is not growing one is dying. Stagnation leads to death.

46. It is not about stumbling and falling down. It is about how long you allow yourself to stay down. The future is not certain. So, why do we look at the negative possibilities instead of looking at the positive possibilities?

47. God does not make mistakes. Remember, *Adversity brings Prosperity* and you get nothing without hard work.

48. Some adults need to learn from babies. Babies love and play with others no matter their race, gender or religion. So if they can do it, why can't you?

49. Every day is a battle. However, each day is the first day of the rest of your life. How are you going to use your days, running from the battles or fighting the battles and making history? The world tells you how to lose. Remember, there were millions of other sperm that were racing to get to that egg. Now here you are! You were born a *Winner*. Don't ever let anyone tell you different.

50. The realest thing you can ever do is to be yourself. Get on it, you will feel much better about life.

51. The devil is all about lies. He did tell one truth, which was, he would try his hardest to make man miserable and lead man astray. You can count on him for that.

52. God loves all and forgives; so why don't you?

53. Your actions do not just affect you. They affect everything around you. Energy is given and energy is received. Be positive, so the energy that you give and receive will be positive.

54. Everyone thinks they are right all the time. Even when they are wrong. If we all acknowledge our wrongs, forgive others for theirs, and realize others are right half the time, it'll be amazing what the world could accomplish; instead of wasting time over petty conflicts which are caused by ego and pride.

55. Remember, although you do not see it all the time, People are always watching you. Your actions may help or harm others so be mindful.

56. Love and appreciate all that you have because in a blink of an eye it can be taken away. When you appreciate the minor things, major things are put in your life.

57. Doubting yourself and others is doubting God. Each breath and each life is a miracle; miracles happen every second.

Epilogue
Till Our Paths Cross Again

Our life courses are parallel to each other. We met at some spot along the way. I have been your teacher and your student. I showed you *Appreciation*, but you took me for granted.

Remember, I showed you *My Love*, and a dedication *To My Son* was born. However, you did not care because *Fear* consumed you, so you did not take a chance on me. I told you *Time* does not wait for anyone, you did not listen. We failed together but in failing we learned what *Success* is. We are at this big party and we are the "in" crowd, but I am the loner in this group. I've been here too long and it's time for me to go. You helped me understand *Who I AM*. Another journey calls.

I am off on my journey. *My Time* has come. Please tell *The Writer and The Pen*, I am not a *Sellout and a Nigger*. Excuse my language I think you understand. Talking to some of you is like having a *Dialog Between the Pessimist and the Optimist*. That's ok; we *Believe* in each other and keep *Shining* together even in our worst times.

One day you will *Remember My Name* and all the *Love* I have for you. Although we wasted much of our time together playing *Hide and Seek*, I do not have any *Regrets*. So do not cry over the times we partied away.

We will cross paths again, sooner or later, only God knows when. Don't worry about me, I will be fine, I am doing well. I bid you all adieu. I love. You all know the rest.

ABOUT THE AUTHOR

Vid Lamonte' Buggs Jr. is a native of Hampton, Virginia whose main goal is to spread motivation, inspiration and love. His work serves to encourage others to look past their differences and focus on uniting to make the world a better place.

He currently resides in Tampa, Florida serving his community as a youth sports coach, mentor and motivational speaker, as well as community activist. While we all face challenges in life, his philosophy is that perseverance, positivity and a heart full of love will enable us to rise above our struggles and become the instruments to spark constructive societal change.

OTHER BOOKS BY
Vid Lamonte' Buggs Jr.

You Ain't Hungry Until I'm Starving – (Available Now at your favorite retailer.)

Getting out of the Dark: How to Have a Life Full of Success, Wealth and Happiness- E-book (Available Now)

It's Cold Out Here, You Need A Coat (Summer 2017)

Vid's Viddles: Volume Two (Winter 2017)

CONNECT WITH VID HERE:

Website: http://www.vidbuggs.com/

Facebook: Vid Lamonte' Buggs Jr.

Twitter: vbuggs

Blog: https://vidsworld.wordpress.com

Instagram: VBUGGS

Youtube: Vid Buggs

4-U-Nique Publishing

Read excerpts, get exclusive inside looks at exciting new titles and authors, find tour schedules and enter contests.

www.4-U-NiquePublishing.com

Need help publishing your masterpiece? We are happy to help.

Email us at info@4-U-NiquePublishing.com

Made in the USA
Columbia, SC
19 November 2017